TEACHING PSYCHOTHERAPY IN CONTEMPORARY PSYCHIATRIC RESIDENCY TRAINING

Report No. 120

TEACHING PSYCHOTHERAPY IN CONTEMPORARY PSYCHIATRIC RESIDENCY TRAINING

Formulated by the Committee on Therapy

Group for the Advancement of Psychiatry

BRUNNER/MAZEL *Publishers* • New York

Library of Congress Cataloging-in-Publication Data

Group for the Advancement of Psychiatry. Committee
on Therapy.
Teaching psychotherapy in contemporary psychiatric
residency training.

(Report; no. 120)
Bibliography: p. 45
1. Psychotherapy—Study and teaching. 2. Psychiatry—
Study and teaching (Residency) I. Title. II. Series:
Report (Group for the Advancement of Psychiatry);
no. 120. [DNLM: 1. Internship and Residency.
2. Psychotherapy—education. W1 RE209BR no. 120 / WM 19.5 G837]

RC321.G7 no. 120 [RC336] 616.89 s 86-26850
ISBN 0-87630-454-4 [616.89'14'0711]

Published by
BRUNNER/MAZEL, INC.
19 Union Square West
New York, New York 10003

MANUFACTURED IN THE UNITED STATES OF AMERICA

STATEMENT OF PURPOSE

THE GROUP FOR THE ADVANCEMENT OF PSYCHIATRY has a membership of approximately 300 psychiatrists, most of whom are organized in the form of a number of working committees. These committees direct their efforts toward the study of various aspects of psychiatry and the application of this knowledge to the fields of mental health and human relations.

Collaboration with specialists in other disciplines has been and is one of GAP's working principles. Since the formation of GAP in 1946 its members have worked closely with such other specialists as anthropologists, biologists, economists, statisticians, educators, lawyers, nurses, psychologists, sociologists, social workers, and experts in mass communication, philosophy, and semantics. GAP envisages a continuing program of work according to the following aims:

1. To collect and appraise significant data in the fields of psychiatry, mental health, and human relations;
2. To reevaluate old concepts and to develop and test new ones;
3. To apply the knowledge thus obtained for the promotion of mental health and good human relations.

GAP is an independent group, and its reports represent the composite findings and opinions of its members only, guided by its many consultants.

TEACHING PSYCHOTHERAPY IN CONTEMPORARY PSYCHIATRIC RESIDENCY TRAINING was formulated by the Committee on Therapy. The members of this committee are listed below. The members of the other GAP committees, as well as additional membership categories and current and past officers of GAP, are listed on pp. 49–56.

Committee on Therapy
Group for the Advancement of Psychiatry

Allan D. Rosenblatt, M.D., Chairperson

Henry Brosin, M.D.
Eugene B. Feigelson, M.D.
Robert Michels, M.D.
Andrew P. Morrison, M.D.
William Offenkrantz, M.D.

Sol W. Ginsberg Fellows
Sharon Weinstein, M.D.
Jane Asch, M.D.

Robert Michels, M.D., served as Chairperson of the Committee during earlier stages of this report

CONTENTS

TEACHING PSYCHOTHERAPY IN CONTEMPORARY PSYCHIATRIC RESIDENCY TRAINING

1

INTRODUCTION

Training and supervised experience in conducting psychotherapy has long been a central theme of psychiatric residency programs, but the role that it plays has changed significantly in the last few decades. Thirty years ago the most respected teachers in psychiatric residency programs were clinicians who were practicing psychoanalysts, and "dynamic" psychotherapy occupied a virtually undisputed pivotal position in psychiatry. Today, in sharp contrast, this traditional centrality of psychotherapy in psychiatric education is being challenged. Both friends and critics are questioning the rationale for teaching psychotherapy in modern psychiatric residency programs, along with the very definition of the profession and the goals of its educational programs. In fact, several current observers are so deeply concerned with the impact of a so-called "identity crisis" in psychiatry and its implications for the future of the profession and the nature of its therapeutic practices, that they have worried about the "survival" of the contemporary resident (and teacher) (Freedman & Gordon, 1973; Osmond, 1973; Yager, 1974; Eaton & Goldstein, 1977; Karasu & Hart, 1979).

Thus, the changing role of psychotherapy in training and in practice cannot be divorced from consideration of the changing scope and context of psychiatry as a whole. Psychiatry has a special place in modern medicine that reflects the ambiguous position it has long tried to occupy as a bridge between the biological and psychosocial aspects of the profession. This intermediary position makes psychiatry peculiarly vulnerable to the vicissitudes of social attitudes and values. As the most psychosocially and least biologically based aspect of psychiatry, psychotherapy and training in it are strongly linked to social, political, and economic forces that shape our world.

These forces and their impact have been discussed both within and outside the discipline. Osmond (1973) described a "siege from within" in which members of the profession advocate widely varied and disparate models of mental illness and its treatment. At the height of the antipsychiatry movement a decade ago, it was even possible to be a psychiatrist in training, affiliation, and status and, at the very same time, an "antipsychiatrist" in ideology and action, rejecting the role of the traditional psychotherapist as well as the other values of the profession. Simultaneously, increasing attention to health care delivery, its cost, and the role of consumers and third parties in health care led to "attacks from without" (Freedman & Gordon, 1973), reflecting public concern and confusion regarding the varied goals, methods, patient populations, and practice settings of the contemporary psychiatrist.

In addressing these issues, we will first highlight those broad sociopolitical as well as scientific changes of the past three decades that have generally affected psychiatric training and practice, especially psychotherapy. In subsequent sections, we will examine the impact of such changes on the teaching of psychotherapy, from the standpoints of what is to be taught, how it is taught, who learns it, and who teaches it.

2

SOCIOPOLITICAL CHANGES

Somers (1977), in her description of the current health scene, concludes:

> There is no question but that the United States is in the midst of the new sociopolitical revolution. . . . Gone is the sense of limitless resources, replaced by a sober appraisal of limited resources. Gone is a one-dimensional approach to causation and cure, replaced by a complex multi-factorial analysis and equally complex prescriptions. . . . Gone is the assumption that the situation can be managed either by private enterprise or by government alone, replaced by a call for a difficult but essential working relationship. . . . Gone also is the idea that the individual consumer has no responsibility, replaced by a call for considerable responsibility and even some sacrifice. (p. 960)

These sweeping alterations of our sociopolitical fabric over the past 30 years are not easily catalogued, nor do they permit simple causal connections to be drawn. The economic aspect includes increasing fiscal stresses, with an increasing awareness of limited resources. The political aspect includes a greater politicalization of medical and psychiatric domains, with the appearance of new interest groups, such as employers, third-party providers, consumer groups, and patients' rights activists. The sociological aspect encompasses a decline of such traditional structures and values as the nuclear family, conventional religious affiliations, and the work ethic, with the growth of alternate family structures, more liberal sexual attitudes, new religious sects, and increased drug use.

Psychiatric manpower shortages identified during World War II led to the development of federal policies featuring greatly increased federal funding intended to encourage psychiatric training programs. It was assumed that increasing the supply of psychiatrists would solve the shortage, and, initially, issues relating to the method and content of training were left in the hands of academic departments of psychiatry. The broader community was relatively indifferent to these developments, since psychiatry was thought of as two professions. One, largely synonymous with psychotherapy and primarily modeled after psychoanalysis, was perceived as elitist or irrelevant by the general public, and the other, symbolized by the large state hospitals that cared for the seriously mentally ill, formed what amounted to a separate system, unrelated to federal concerns, academic programs, or the career goals of psychiatric residents.

In this setting of strong professional allegiance to the intellectual traditions of psychoanalysis, governmental financial support for psychiatric education, and an indifferent or at least laissez faire attitude by the general community, training institutions emphasized the teaching of long-term exploratory psychotherapy as central to the curriculum of psychiatric residencies. Students who entered these programs often saw psychiatric training as a preliminary step toward becoming a psychoanalyst or psychoanalytic psychotherapist (Lewin & Ross, 1960).

With the postwar expansion of psychiatric training in high gear, the introduction of modern psychotropic drugs in the late 1950s was accompanied by sweeping changes in psychiatric practice, eventually challenging the primacy of psychoanalytic psychotherapy in American psychiatry. The symptomatic control of the acute psychoses facilitated the subsequent emergence of therapeutic communities and milieu programs in psychiatric hospitals, and the discharge of patients from large public hospitals obliged psychiatrists to develop new programs for maintaining them in the community. General psychiatrists began to see more chronic and often more disturbed patients in outpatient settings. This process was also catalyzed by the report of the 1961 Joint Congressional Commission on Mental Illness, a blueprint for the emerging community mental health movement and a "bold new approach" to mental illness.

This new public health focus in psychiatry became associated with a growing demand to treat more patients and to develop more effective methods of treatment, symptom-focused, supportive, or crisis-oriented, rather than directed toward character change and personal growth. It also shifted therapeutic attention away from more affluent and sophisticated patients—the characteristic recipients of psychoanalytic treatments—to the socially disadvantaged, poor, and underserved minorities. This new "social" focus, with its increased number of patients, also involved an extension of the therapist role to nonphysicians. The psychiatrist became only one of a team of mental health professionals and paraprofessionals involved in treating patients within a broadened concept of comprehensive mental health services.

As these new goals for psychiatry crystallized, some mental health professionals began to regard psychoanalytic psychotherapy as having only limited usefulness. There was less interest in intrapsychic change and more concern with behavioral and social parameters. There was a shift in focus from the individuals to the social system—family, group, and community. The "social" wave in psychiatry also led to the development of an array of modalities and techniques of psychosocial intervention (family, marital, and peer group treatments, community outreach programs, etc.).

The emergence of behavior modification therapies represented another divergence from psychodynamic approaches. Other schools of psychotherapy aimed not at behavioral change per se, but rather at an attitudinal and philosophical restructuring, as in the "cognitive therapy" of depression. Finally, "experiential" schools of therapy, in contrast to both dynamic and behavioral schools, sought arousal, emotion, and experience, rather than cognition, insight, or action.

The proliferation of clinical programs and therapeutic modalities, along with the growth of patient populations and of health care costs in general, laid the groundwork for the rapid escalation of mental health costs. Government, the community, patients, and insurance companies, as well as psychotherapists themselves, began to raise questions about the efficacy, appropriateness, and cost-effectiveness of psychotherapeutic techniques, compared to alternative psychiatric treatments.

Federal goals shifted from stimulating the training of more psychiatrists to controlling the costs of psychiatric care. There is now significant government interest in the content of curricula, with periodic revisions of "priorities" that are defined in terms of perceived social needs (and politically popular themes), rather than theoretical or scientific schools. Residency programs are thus expected to be primarily concerned with certain defined patient populations, e.g., the poor, disadvantaged, handicapped, children, the elderly, minorities, chronic patients, or substance abusers, rather than with issues of psychoanalysis, behaviorism, neurobiology, or social sciences. The government has been more concerned with what psychiatrists do, where they do it, to whom they do it, how much it costs, and what impact it has on other institutions, rather than simply assuming that there is a shortage of psychiatrists, that we should train more, and that the profession can be trusted to define its own role and to expend the resources made available to it. The shameful state of the state hospitals, previously largely ignored by the profession as well as the public, came to serve as a dramatic symbol of the dangers in allowing a profession to solve its own problems. (For the role of government in mental health care, see Brown, 1985; Foley & Sharfstein, 1983; Grob, 1983; Levine, 1981; and Rothman, 1979.)

The elaboration of multiple social and biochemical models of illness and the associated techniques of treatment has created an awesome body of knowledge for residents (and teachers) to master and integrate. Residents are affected by competing ideologies and role models, as well as by the cultural and social values of their contemporaries. Administrators and teachers in residency programs, affected by community and governmental concerns regarding cost-effectiveness, efficacy, and social relevance, struggle with conflicts between service and educational needs in assigning priorities within the teaching programs.

The end result of these converging social, political, economic, and scientific changes has been a diminished scope for dynamic psychotherapy as the primary modality of psychiatric treatment. Thus, neither treatments nor patients nor settings nor teachers nor residents are the same as they were three decades ago. In the subsequent sections we will examine these differences.

3

CHANGES IN WHAT IS TO BE TAUGHT

Modalities of Psychotherapy

In the course of its evolution from Freud's proverbial "talking cure," the scope of formal psychotherapy has been vastly expanded. The field has undergone a virtual explosion of therapeutic modalities from orthodox Freudian psychoanalysis through "Neo-Freudian" dynamic approaches to non-Freudian (i.e., nondynamic) techniques. In addition, a variety of nonindividual formats have evolved, e.g., marital, family, small-group, and large-group encounters.

To attempt here any further classification and discussion of all the current modalities and formats would go far beyond the scope of this document. The interested reader is referred to a number of comprehensive surveys and studies (Frances, Clarkin, & Perry, 1984; Karasu & Bellak, 1980; Karasu, et al., 1984; Kovel, 1976; Lewis & Usdin, 1982; Smith, Glass & Miller, 1980).

A generation ago, the resident had only to develop some familiarity and beginning competence with supportive therapy and insight-directed therapeutic endeavors. Today he or she is expected to learn about supportive therapies, dynamic therapies, behavior modification therapies, marital and family therapies, group therapies, etc. There is just not enough time to acquire adequate supervised experience in all modalities and formats. Moreover, competing theories and techniques tend to be presented with little attempt to discern commonalities or complementary aspects. Thus, the resident often is provided no opportunity to appreciate, for example, the role of transference in behavior modification therapies or the role of conditioning in dynamic psychotherapies.

There has been a growth of interest in the possibility that systematic scientific research on psychotherapy will have an influence on both practice and teaching (Michels, 1985). Most of the research up to now has focused on outcome and has had more impact on the politics and economics of psychotherapy than on practice or teaching. More recently, several groups have been studying the therapeutic process, and manuals describing specific therapies have been developed (Klerman, Weissman, Rounsaville, & Chevron, 1984; Luborsky, 1984; Strupp & Binder, 1984). However, to date these have had little impact on the way that psychotherapy is actually practiced or taught. Of course, this is hardly surprising, since this type of research requires an unusually long time for results to be meaningful. The manual approach does have potential implications for pedagogic strategy, but at this point these have barely been considered. The manuals available at present were developed to be used by skilled therapists in order to ensure the reliability of the therapies they employ in research studies, rather than to teach psychotherapy to beginners. There is no reason to believe that the therapies they describe are better or worse than any other therapies. Furthermore, many teachers of therapy believe that there are inherent drawbacks to a manual approach when teaching beginners (Michels, 1985).

New Patterns of Psychopathology

There have been marked alterations in patterns of psychopathology reported in Western industrialized countries within the last 30 years. Some contend that these reflect only a change of diagnostic fashion or definition (Loomie, 1972;

Blum, 1978), but others argue that they represent "real" changes in prevalence of underlying psychopathology (Kohut, 1971; Loewald, 1971; Giovacchini, 1975), presumably a consequence of sociocultural influences (Keniston, 1970; Lowenfeld & Lowenfeld, 1970; Kovel, 1976; Lasch, 1979). Whatever the explanation, the patients seen by psychiatric residents are different from those seen several decades ago, or at least are perceived differently. These progressive changes in psychopathology over time have been reported for both inpatient (Blum, 1978) and outpatient (Lazar, 1973) populations.

Blum (1978) compared samples of inpatients discharged in 1954, 1964, and 1974 and reported three major trends. Within the 20-year period, the rate of diagnoses of affective disorder tripled, that of schizophrenia increased significantly, and that of neuroses dropped from the highest to the lowest. Lazar (1973) surveyed outpatients within a comparable 20-year period and found that in 1952 there were four times as many symptom neuroses as personality disorders, but by 1959 the two groups were equal, and by 1971 the order was reversed, with twice as many personality disorders as symptom neuroses.

Blum speculated that one reason for these trends may have been an increase in the utilization of

> diagnostic categories more consistent with biological treatment (e.g., affective disorders and schizophrenia) and a decrease in the ascription of categories less appropriate to this model (e.g., neuroses). (p. 1017)

This would parallel the trend in psychiatry away from a psychodynamic psychotherapeutic perspective and toward a psychopharmacological one.

Not only has there been a shift from symptom neuroses to personality disorders, but within the personality disorder group, there has been a significant increase in narcissistic, borderline, and related disorders. The most prominent clinical features have been described as

> problems related to aggression; impoverishment of affect and avoidance of commitment; permanent adolescence with fading of adulthood as an aim; omnipotent and narcissistic expectations; superego defects and conflict; impaired ego-ideal function; regressive phenomena; defective sense of identity; feelings of alienation and unrelatedness, . . . and a compelling need for change, action, movement, immediacy, and fluidity (Lazar, 1973). (pp. 585–586)

Although Lazar's findings are taken from a predominantly white upper-middle-class population, other phenomena point to similar changes affecting all socioeconomic strata. The explosion of the "drug culture" in the past two decades has resulted in dramatic increases in numbers of pathological patterns related to addiction and drug abuse, with their related episodes of drug overdose. Moreover, epidemiological surveys reveal that the incidence of suicide in adolescents and young adults more than doubled in the decade of the sixties, alone (O'Brien, 1977).

Whatever the underlying explanations for these changes in perceived clinical picture, a significant portion of the resident's current case load is subsumed under diagnostic categories (e.g., borderline and narcissistic personality disorders) that were hardly delineated 30 years ago. Furthermore, the popular psychodynamic formulations of those times, centering around Oedipal-level conflicts and more mature defensive processes, are not the dominant framework for understanding these patients. New dynamic concepts, involving early object relations, primitive defenses, such as splitting, and early self-object representations, must be included in the resident's theoretical vocabulary, within a developmental framework that encompasses patterns of developmental arrest and consequent structural deficits so prominent in such cases.

In practice, the first case assigned to a resident for intensive outpatient psychotherapy is often a severe narcissistic or borderline personality disorder. The primitive emotionality, arrogance or clinging demandingness, and related clinical characteristics of such patients, coupled with their ability to evoke intense countertransference responses, frequently make therapeutic encounters with them a trying experience even for skilled and experienced therapists. For a beginning resident, even with competent supervision, such an experience can be painful and discouraging, coloring future attitudes toward psychotherapy.

In addition to these changes in the prevalence of pathological entities (or changes in diagnostic fashion), the public's conception of what constitutes mental illness and its expectations of what psychotherapy has to offer have also changed. This, in turn, has influenced who seeks psychiatric help and therefore whom residents are trained to treat. Psychiatry's own view of mental illness is, of course, an important factor in this process, and definitions of mental illness have progressively broadened in recent years. For example, a generation or so ago it would have been much more unlikely for anyone to consult a psychiatrist for marital difficulties, unsatisfying interpersonal relationships, or problems in making commitments. Not only are such patients common today, but psychiatrists may encounter patients who look upon any reduction of personal potential as an indication for psychotherapy, who think of health as the fullest realization of self (mind, body, and spirit), and who regard psychotherapy (not necessarily conducted by psychiatrists alone) as appropriate for everyone as an aid in coping with the psychic stresses of human existence.

Patient Population and Treatment Settings

In addition to changes in psychopathology and in types of treatment, there have been changes in the populations served by psychiatrists and in the clinical settings in which they are seen. The current psychiatry resident faces the challenge of providing psychiatric treatment in settings not traditionally identified with the practice of psychotherapy, such as emergency rooms, general-hospital wards, community mental health centers, street clinics, social agencies, and schools.

The expected roles in these new settings differ from the traditional role of the psychotherapist. Extraclinical contacts may involve interaction with the legal system, social service agencies, police, schools, and welfare offices. The resident may have to relinquish hard-won professional status when functioning in nonpsychiatric settings. Yet, at the same time his or her work in these settings may be misunderstood or devalued by the more traditional supervisors, who thus unwittingly contribute to already ambiguous and conflicting expectations (Morrison et al., 1973). Work in these new contexts, in which the resident may be simultaneously acting as therapist, patient advocate, and organizational consultant, also has brought new questions about the boundaries of the profession to the foreground of training. Is the psychiatrist's role to be limited to the traditional passive receptive one of working with patients who approach him for consultation and treatment? Or is the psychiatrist to expand his role in terms of outreach, assertively creating therapeutic contracts with public agencies or private corporations and in other ways altering the traditional stance of the psychiatric physician?

The many new settings in which the resident works and the types of patients whom he or she treats are often unfamiliar to the teachers, who may be little prepared to help the resident deal with the chronic schizophrenic in the halfway house or the obstreperous agitator in a neighborhood health clinic. Karasu et al. (1978) have correctly urged that supervision should be oriented to the actual tasks that residents will be asked to undertake. However, paradoxically, the problems that the resident faces in the training setting may have little relevance to those clinical tasks he or she anticipates as central to his or her future career. Greben (1976) notes that much residency training takes place in settings where there is little emphasis on psychotherapy; yet, for the majority of residents, psychotherapy is a significant theme of their future professional lives. Thus, relatively little time is spent teaching psychiatric residents the work that will occupy much of their future.

For instance, a resident may be doing much of his or her PGY-III training in outpatient psychiatry in a court clinic setting. The psychotherapy patients may be referred by probation officers or the court clerk with the understanding not only that psychotherapy is mandatory for probation, but also that the resident should cure the patients' antisocial behavior, which, after all, has led to the arrests. Such a specialized clientele is very limiting in terms of the range of patients available for learning psychotherapy techniques. In addition, our resident's supervisor may be a psychoanalyst, trained in the outpatient clinic attached to the psychoanalytic institute in the same city, who has had limited experience working within the legal system and, despite good will toward the resident supervisee and his or her patients, is perplexed by the psychopathology presented and the expectations inherent in the court setting.

4

CHANGES IN METHODS OF TEACHING

Supervision

The most common, most important, and probably most effective method of teaching psychotherapy is by means of supervision. This generally consists of regular meetings between student and supervisor, during which the student reports on an ongoing treatment and the supervisor discusses it. There is an extensive literature on supervisory teaching, primarily in reference to the teaching of psychoanalysis, but also of psychotherapy and even of diagnostic interviewing. (See, for example, Caligor, 1984; Eckstein & Wallerstein, 1972; Fleming & Benedek, 1966; and Schuster, Sandt, & Thaler, 1972.)

Supervision may focus on the patient's pathology or psychodynamics, on the therapeutic process, or on the therapist's experience and functioning. Optimally, it shifts back and forth among these, depending on the nature of the clinical and educational problems, the interest and skill of the supervisee and the supervisor, and the phase of both the therapy and the supervision. There are often times when it is important that the supervisor explore how the resident's psychological conflicts interfere with his or her performance as a therapist. This may have a therapeutic effect, but that should be incidental to its educational intent. Supervision should not be therapy, although it may be therapeutic, and at times it may lead to recognition of the need for therapy, with the suggestion that it be considered.

Supervision may vary in its primary aim, which might range from teaching interpersonal sensitivity (i.e., the use of empathy), to psychotherapeutic technique, to using the resident's own evoked emotional responses as therapeutic tools, to identifying and exploring more narrowly defined countertransference problems. Supervision can be used for evaluative as well as educational goals, and there is considerable discussion regarding when these goals are competitive, compatible, or facilitative.

There is a tendency for the supervisory process to mirror the therapeutic process, and this can be used as an opportunity for the exploration of issues that arise in the therapeutic situation (Arlow, 1963; Sachs & Shapiro, 1976; Gediman & Wolkenfeld, 1980). Supervision can be individual or in groups, with a tendency for the structure of supervision to parallel the structure of treatment, with individual psychotherapy supervised in individual sessions, group psychotherapy supervised in groups, and even some experiments with therapists bringing their families to training sessions in family therapy. The supervisory situation may be manipulated for other reasons as well. For example, the presence of several trainees can inhibit a more intrusive or psychotherapeutic posture on the part of the supervisor, or less frequent supervisory discussions can shift attention away from details of technique to more global issues.

The availability of modern technology for recording psychotherapeutic sessions has raised interesting educational problems and has also reawakened old questions regarding the appropriate substrate for the supervisory process. Studies have regularly demonstrated that the therapy session as reported by a supervisee is quite different from the session as directly observed by a third party or recorded by a camera (Schuster et al., 1972). For some, this argues for the value of direct recording to enrich the database for supervision. For others, the basis of supervision is the therapist's experience; its incongruence with the view of an external observer is assumed. Any attempt to sidestep the supervisory confrontation with the therapist's personal interpretation and transformation of the therapeutic process is viewed as an interference with the essential function of supervision. The issue reflects the same controversy in psychotherapy. Some believe that the distortions in the patient's account of his world should lead the therapist to explore the world directly, as by meeting the important people in the patient's life. Others assert that such distortions should be seen as the central field of inquiry in a psychotherapy, where the patient's strategy for constructing his personal world can best be understood when the therapist avoids any contamination that will lead him to construct an alternate world of the therapist rather than understanding the patient's. Nor surprisingly, therapists who advocate one or the other approach tend to become supervisors who advocate the analogous approach.

Despite the polar advocates in this controversy about "objective" versus "subjective" supervisory approaches, there are educators who believe the two are not incompatible. Videotapes of sessions are periodically studied with the resident, in addition to the regular use of process notes, as a useful means of broadening the resident's awareness of his or her role, both objective and experiential, in the therapeutic process.

Didactic Teaching

Didactic teaching also has a role in psychodynamic psychotherapeutic training. Generally, this is of two main types. One is the teaching of a human psychology, such as psychoanalytic theory, that is expected to guide the understanding and the interventions of the psychotherapist. The other is the teaching of the theory and practice of therapeutic technique. At times, these two subjects are surprisingly disconnected in psychotherapy. Many, perhaps most, programs emphasize the first, and most of the literature in the field is devoted to it. (One exception is a recent APA publication, *Treatment Planning in Psychiatry,* Lewis & Usdin, 1982, in which the chapter "Psychodynamic Treatment Planning" integrates a psychodynamic model of behavior with various modalities of psychodynamic psychotherapy.) Not surprisingly, most trainees value the teaching of practical technique and seek out teachers who can convey it without being simplistic or platitudinous.

Teachers are often concerned lest the teaching of technique lead to a superficial imitation rather than a thoughtful application of personal understanding; students often feel that while theory may help them to organize their observations, they are left not knowing what to do with patients. Still another point of view is that didactic teaching alone of either type is of little assistance, that theoretical understanding must grow from personal clinical experience if it is to have meaning. In this view, although supervision can help a student to develop that understanding from his or her experience, didactic teaching that is not based on the student's personal clinical experience is likely to create barriers to the true appreciation and understanding of that experience.

Case Conferences and Group Teaching

Case conferences, particularly continuous case conferences, are in some ways intermediate between supervision and didactic teaching. They have the advantage of clinical immediacy in a seminarlike context, but they sometimes have the disadvantage of the diminished attention and interest that beginning students experience in listening to the often bewildering data of the clinical experience of others. Clarity is educational, and resolving one's own confusion is particularly educational, but participating in the confusion of others can be problematic.

In this respect, technological advances have also widened pedagogical options from those available 30 years ago. Residents may now watch a supervisor or other experienced and skilled therapist actually treat a patient through one-way mirrors or videotape recordings. This can be particularly fruitful when the therapist is available to share his or her inner experiences with the residents, supplementing their observations of the therapy as viewed from outside the therapist. Some educators believe that despite the danger of shallow, unthinking imitation, it is useful for beginning therapists to see a model in action that they can imitate, at least early on. It is hoped that such imitation will lead to selective identification and autonomous functioning.

On the other hand, it may be argued that since beginning residents are most prone to use global identification with an instructor, including his perhaps idiosyncratic behavior, to cope with their anxieties, such viewing of ongoing therapy should be reserved for later in training. At that time, it may be helpful for residents to observe that even the most revered of mentors cannot be "perfect" therapists.

Whether by case conference, viewing ongoing therapy, or group supervision, group teaching can act to ameliorate anxieties provoked in the one-to-one interaction with a supervisor. In individual supervision, the beginning resident must repeatedly confront his or her errors, even if supported by an ideally empathic supervisor. These injuries to self-esteem cannot always be adequately dealt with without the undesirable transformation of the supervision into treatment. In a group setting (even as small as two), each resident may be able to compare personal experience and feelings with those of peers and thereby feel less inadequate. Group process may also permit the participants to challenge more openly the instructor's theoretical bias, whether it be psychoanalysis or behaviorism, thus allowing for a healthy intellectual exchange, as well as a relief of the tension provoked by their feelings of inadequacy. Finally, the use of group teaching permits residents to be exposed to a wider range of clinical phenomena and issues than is available through their individual experiences.

5
CHANGES IN THE RESIDENTS

Decline in Popularity of Psychiatry

Even while psychiatry has been expanding its theoretical foundation, clinical application, and populations served, it has declined in popularity among medical students as a career choice (Gurel, 1973, 1976; Nielsen, 1979, 1980; Reinhold, 1980). The number of medical school graduates who select psychiatric training has decreased both in absolute number and in percentage of total graduates. The projections of national requirements for physicians made by the Graduate Medical Education National Advisory Committee indicate that adult and child psychiatry will continue to be medical specialties whose practitioners are in short supply, in sharp contrast to others, such as internal medicine, general surgery, and obstetrics and gynecology, which are expected to be oversupplied with physicians within the next 10 years (Reinhold, 1980).

Nielsen (1979) attributed the decline in the popularity of psychiatry among medical students to shifts in the characteristics of applicants admitted to medical schools, the impact of the medical school experience, changes in medical curricula, the attitudes of medical students about psychiatry and its role in medicine, and the competing appeal presented by primary-care specialties. In addition, it is possible that many psychiatrists selected their specialty because of its psychotherapeutic orientation, and that as that theme has diminished in psychiatry, it has become less attractive to many medical students. A later study (Nielsen & Eaton, 1981) suggested the importance of medical school psychiatric education in influencing career decisions. It was found that psychiatric curricula that provided the student with more clinical responsibility and more time for close contact with psychiatric teachers produced students who felt more positive about the specialty of psychiatry and were thus more likely to choose it as a career. The discrepancy in anticipated future financial rewards is becoming an increasingly important determinant of medical student choice since the trend toward decreasing psychiatric coverage and reimbursement by third-party payors.

The impact of the diminished pool of American medical graduate applicants for psychiatric training is aggravated by limitations on the number of foreign medical graduates entering this country and the simultaneous decrease in federal support for psychiatric education. These trends are occurring at the time of predicted increases in the demand both for direct psychiatric services (National Institute of Mental Health, 1976; Goldberg et al., 1976; Doyle, 1978; Pardes, 1979) and for consultative and educational services to nonpsychiatric physicians (Eaton & Goldstein, 1977; Regier, Goldberg, & Taube, 1978; Haupt, Orleans, George, et al., 1979). This heightened demand is related to the growing recognition of the public health dimensions of psychiatric illness and of the role of psychosocial factors in all forms of illness.

Increased Diversity of Students

Even though their numbers are diminished, the students who choose psychiatry today constitute an even more heterogeneous group than before. At least three distinct subgroups can be identified. The first is reminiscent of those students of the past who made their commitment to psychiatry well before entering medical school. They were attracted by those psychological concerns of psychiatry that differentiate it from the rest of clinical medicine and had little interest in that basic medical curriculum. The second subgroup generally does not consider psychiatry before medical school, shows greater interest in the general medical curriculum, and is characterized as having a "general practitioner" orientation (Nemetz & Weiner, 1965). These are the students who are interested in caring for the "whole patient" and who may have shifted their specialty choice from family practice to psychiatry. The third subgroup, much smaller, but often highly valued by academic training programs and therefore important in the sociology of psychiatric education, is stimulated by the emerging neurobiological emphasis of modern psychiatry and selects it as a field that is about to undergo the explosive growth of research and new knowledge that has marked internal medicine in the past few decades.

Notwithstanding this diversity and despite the diminished emphasis on psychotherapy in the current psychiatric milieu, most residents consider the role of psychotherapy in their training, future career, and personal lives to be of critical concern. Attitudes toward the arduous task of learning to "do" psychotherapy are shaped by a variety of factors, including personal qualities, experiences, and values instilled by the training institution, as well as the larger socioeconomic issues.

Factors Influencing Attitude Toward Psychotherapy

The resident's approach to learning psychotherapy is often colored by prior contact with it, sometimes occurring before entering residency. Some residents have had personal psychotherapy before they chose psychiatry as a specialty. For them, the selection of psychiatry may in part represent an identification with their personal therapists, and their high evaluation of psychotherapy may reflect more of a transference response than an objective assessment. Other personal experiences that may lead to an unrealistic valuation of psychotherapy include identification with a family member who is a psychotherapist or a relationship with a family member who has been treated with psychotherapy.

Early in training, residents generally have the opportunity to "sit with patients," most often inpatients with psychoses or severe character disorders. Although some trainees derive great satisfaction from this experience, others, particularly those working on short-term inpatient units, observe that medication has quicker and more dramatic effects. This observation may dissuade some residents from trying to learn psychotherapy, especially if they do not have a strong prior commitment to its value.

The values of the institution also affect residents' interest in psychotherapy. The residents beginning training in the eighties may find themselves in a setting in which biological and psychosocial perspectives are polarized. Different factions among the faculty compete for grants, patients, the residents' service time, and ideological support. Residents often feel torn by these competing orientations and may feel compelled to choose an orientation prematurely, thus foreclosing areas of enrichment and intellectual exploration. Skepticism about the efficacy of psychotherapy may discourage residents from the hard work necessary to acquire the skill.

Attitudes toward psychotherapy training during residency are inextricably linked to the resident's perception of his or her future career goals. These goals are, in turn, influenced by a multiplicity of external pressures. Questions about life-style, including family, finances, geographic location, and schedules, may be overriding factors as residents think about their future directions. The resident in his or her late twenties or early thirties is attempting to integrate career goals with desires for intimacy and family life. He or she must weigh, for example, the advantages of greater flexibility in schedule for the psychotherapist against the advantages of greater income potential for the more biologically oriented psychiatrist practicing in a hospital setting. The income differential between these positions may be considerable, and recognition that the practice of psychotherapy may require financial sacrifices is demoralizing to trainees. For most residents, "moonlighting" has become a fact of life; many of these jobs are in hospitals where the major mode of treatment is psychopharmacological. Experiences in such institutions may not only diminish any psychotherapeutic inclinations, but may be so professionally disappointing as to provoke consideration of alternate career paths.

Economic concerns also influence residents' decisions about obtaining personal therapy or analysis during residency, in the past a common adjunct to the institutional curriculum. As access to third-party payments decreases, fewer residents may pursue the intensive psychotherapy or psychoanalysis once considered a training desideratum.

Another factor discouraging residents from interest in psychotherapy may be the anticipation of significant competition for patients, especially in major urban settings. As more practitioners of other mental health disciplines enter the market place as psychotherapists, residents perceive their own "turf" to be diminishing. However, the perception of competitive issues may vary, depending on the gender of the resident. Psychotherapy patients are predominantly female, and in today's world many have been influenced by the feminist movement of the 1960s and 1970s. As a result, female residents may be more confident about their eventual ability to build up a private practice, while males have an additional concern.

Residents often assume the role of "medical backup" or administrator to nurses, psychologists, and social workers who are delivering primary mental health services. Through such experiences, their professional identities as psychiatrists may come to rest on more traditional "medical" and even administrative skills rather than on their psychotherapeutic abilities. Some residents conclude that physicians have no place in the practice of psychotherapy and that mere "talk" is the domain of the other disciplines. Residents committed to becoming psychotherapists or psychoanalysts may experience considerable discouragement as they find themselves questioning their major purpose in entering the field.

Residents aspiring to academic careers notice that the number of psychoanalysts and psychotherapists in such positions has diminished drastically in recent years. Faculty role models are more often laboratory scientists or clinical administrators, who may not even have an interest in clinical psychiatry, let alone psychotherapy. Economic concerns, schedule demands, and academic procedures make it increasingly difficult to combine a psychotherapeutic practice with a research career in an academic setting, and the choice between the two is often made before the end of residency.

Despite all the forces discouraging an emphasis on learning psychotherapy during residency training, many residents are deeply fascinated by and absorbed in the process of acquiring this difficult skill. However, this group of residents is increasingly paying the price of decreased professional self-esteem and pessimism about future prestige and material success within their chosen specialty.

6

CHANGES IN THE TEACHERS

Changing Role of Analyst–Teacher

Most teachers of psychotherapy in psychiatry residency programs are themselves psychiatrists who have subspecialized in psychotherapy, as either an exclusive or a primary professional activity. Often the most prestigious and sought-after teachers are psychoanalysts, and not uncommonly they are called upon to teach a form of psychotherapy that is different from the mode of therapy that they themselves practice—briefer, perhaps less exploratory and more supportive, and less like psychoanalysis. In a time when the average American psychoanalyst has fewer analytic hours in his or her practice than he or she would like, there may be a tendency to shape the supervisee's therapy into an analytic mode, thus fulfilling the supervisor's wish to practice psychoanalysis vicariously.

Today's psychotherapy teachers are likely to have a somewhat different role in the residency training program than they had two or three decades ago. They are likely to be voluntary or part-time members of the faculty, with the remainder of their time devoted to the private practice of psychotherapy, as was true in the past. However, full-time academic psychiatrists, most of whose orientation is neither psychodynamic nor psychotherapeutic, are becoming increasingly dominant in residency training programs. The result is that, although the average teacher of psychotherapy continues to represent the same pattern of professional activity as in the past, the world around him or her and the other members of the faculty has changed, so that he or she is now different from most of the leaders of the residency program. This change does not necessarily lead to conflict, but it can promote tension and the sense that there are mutually exclusive pathways that lead either to careers in the private practice of psychodynamic psychotherapy or to the full-time pursuit of biologically oriented academic psychiatry.

In many of the more prestigious academic training programs, the picture is further complicated because the director of training is more closely identified with the psychodynamic-psychotherapeutic paradigm than are most other members of the full-time faculty. This can lead to splits that not only separate core from peripheral faculty, but also divide the core faculty, itself, and may extend to the residency group. In such splits, one segment of the residents, usually the larger one, identifies with the training director, the supervisors, and private practice, while the other (often more highly regarded) group moves closer to the majority of the core full-time faculty, consequently feeling in conflict about psychodynamic psychotherapy.

Many of today's teachers of psychotherapy were themselves trained in an era when psychotherapy was the dominant theme of psychiatry and when residents who did not plan careers that centered upon it were viewed as deviant. Attitudes that were appropriate, or at least common, in this earlier era may not be appropriate today. Teachers' attitudes may also be colored by concerns about their own careers. Surveys of psychoanalysts have suggested that many are troubled by not experiencing the demand for their services that they had anticipated, and the relative decrease in income of psychiatrists compared to other medical specialists is well known. In brief, when today's teachers of psychotherapy were students, they saw themselves, and were seen by others, as the best of the profession. Today they are no longer certain of that role, and that shift has an impact on the educational climate.

Nonphysician Teachers

Psychotherapy is widely practiced by nonphysicians, a number of whom have been particularly prominent in the development and teaching of many specialized types of psychotherapy, e.g., group, family, marital, sex, child, etc. The growing tendency to teach psychotherapy in terms of these specific strategies is associated with an increased prevalence of nonphysician teachers. Moreover, many of the leaders in the growing field of psychotherapy research are nonphysician psychotherapists. As a result, residents are not only trained in psychotherapy by physician–psychotherapists of somewhat lower status than in the past, they are also more likely than before to be trained in psychotherapy by nonphysicians. The increasing presence of such nonmedical mentors in the context of the current climate tends to further stimulate conflicts between their identity as physicians and that as psychotherapists.

7

PROPOSALS FOR THE FUTURE

Functions of Psychotherapy Training

In view of the changes that have been discussed here, what is the future role of training in psychotherapy for residents? There are those who advocate abandoning all such training (Detre & Weinberger, 1985; Kroll, 1986). Psychotherapy, they say, should be left to the nonmedical disciplines, such as psychology and social work, while psychiatry should be restricted to its "biological" compass. At the other extreme, some advocate extensive training in psychotherapy as the keystone of psychiatry for all residents. To delineate more clearly just where psychotherapy training should fit into future residency training, we must examine what functions are performed by this training.

Psychotherapy training here refers primarily to supervision in the conduct of psychotherapy, along with seminars that are designed to explore the theoretical bases of the clinical activities. Such supervision and instruction can be separated from the teaching of psychodynamics and psychopathology as basic sciences, these being analogous to physiology and pathology in medical training. They are obviously both prerequisites for training in psychotherapy, but they may be taught to a limited extent without teaching psychotherapy. (To what extent this is feasible without clinical exposure is a matter to which we will return.)

With this in mind, we can identify at least three functions

that are performed by training in psychotherapy. First, a set of skills based on a body of knowledge is taught, one that is indispensable to becoming a practicing psychotherapist. True, not all psychiatry residents will become psychotherapists. Yet these skills in understanding and dealing with distressed people are necessary for the optimal practice of other modalities of therapy, such as pharmacotherapy or behavior modification therapy. Examples would be the ability to perceive that a schizophrenic patient may stop taking medication in response to fears of engulfment or in an attempt to be returned to the hospital with its nurturant care, and the knowledge to predict that a patient may respond more readily to one program of "shaping" behavior than to another, because it offers more opportunity to identify with the therapist.

Second, the process of psychotherapy itself acts as a vital laboratory for the acquisition of essential knowledge. An attempt to teach psychodynamics without psychotherapeutic experience is equivalent to an attempt to teach human anatomy without dissection. One can describe phenomena to a student, but he cannot see and experience them for himself—an essential pedagogical requirement.

Third, training in psychotherapy facilitates a set of attitudes. These attitudes include:

1. A readiness to attend to all aspects of individual communicative behavior, including covert as well as overt, paralinguistic and kinesic as well as linguistic, and omissions or apparent irrelevancies as well as relevant content.
2. A readiness to adopt a nonjudgmental attitude of attentive, "active," empathic listening and observation in the face of a wide range of feelings in the patient.
3. A readiness to employ one's own evoked emotional responses as sensitive diagnostic tools.

4. A readiness to consider multiple and hidden motivations to account for behavior.
5. A readiness to consider and integrate a patient's transference attitudes and responses into a total therapeutic plan, regardless of the therapeutic modality employed.
6. A readiness to consider a patient as a whole person within a biopsychosocial context, whose suffering is to be alleviated without undue compromise of autonomy. Although family and general practitioners are returning to the once commonplace awareness of the patient as a whole person, nowhere else but in psychiatry is the value of the patient's autonomy taught so explicitly and with such emphasis.

Finally, for many trainees, the experience of doing psychotherapy is an important event in their professional socialization as psychiatrists, in much the same way that dissecting a cadaver is an important socializing experience for medical students into medicine.

Basic Training Versus Subspecialty Training

It is clear that psychotherapy is no longer synonymous with psychiatry, but rather is a subspecialty in a broader field. It is also clear, then, that a resident who chooses to become primarily a practicing psychotherapist will require more training in the skills of psychotherapy than one who does not so choose.

The teaching of psychotherapy, however, provides every resident with a framework within which he or she can not only acquire valuable knowledge and skills, but also integrate a set of attitudes necessary for competent functioning in many areas of psychiatry. The knowledge acquired by a psychotherapeutically trained clinical psychiatrist becomes an invaluable adjunct to other modalities of psychiatric treatment. The clinical psychiatric investigator, so trained, is better able to consider psychodynamic variables. In short, the psychotherapeutically trained psychiatrist has an advantage over the psychiatrist without such training, in that he or she has a qualitatively different way in which to order his or her view of the world. This is true whether he or she be a clinician, researcher, administrator, or educator.

Viewed from this perspective, the question of the future role of training in psychotherapy for residents is not an ideological one of whether or not such training is appropriate, but a pragmatic one of how much psychotherapy training is required to accomplish these basic educational goals for the resident who is not being trained to become a practicing psychotherapist. The answer to this question can only come through experience. Psychiatric educators, however, must distinguish between the broader integrative and attitudinal goals of psychotherapy training and the narrower "skill-training" goals that characterize curricula designed to train future psychotherapists, so that appropriate criteria may be developed to evaluate varied training programs.

To accomplish both sets of goals, it is important that those who teach and supervise psychotherapy be experienced psychotherapists who are able not only to instruct in specific skills, but to promote an integration of knowledge and the attitudes discussed above. It is helpful, whenever possible, for supervisors to represent psychotherapy models that are not exclusively psychodynamic, e.g., behavioral, existential, etc. The resident thereby gains a broader view of the commonalities present in all forms of psychotherapy and learns to bring psychodynamic understanding to bear on those practices that do not include dynamically unconscious motives in their theories. Finally, those psychodynamically oriented teachers should explicitly understand and be able to communicate the differences as well as the similarities among the various modalities of psychodynamic psychotherapy.

Value of Personal Therapy

Until recent years, the value of personal therapy for the aspiring psychotherapist has been virtually unquestioned. Today, given the eclectic goals of the trainees and of the training institutions, plus the considerable cost to the resident in both time and money, personal therapy during the residency years is no longer so staunchly advocated. There is a paucity of reported research about the usefulness of personal therapy and none about its usefulness in the training of psychiatrists of other than psychoanalytic orientation (Greenberg & Staller, 1981). There is no hard evidence that psychotherapists who have undergone psychotherapy will be more successful as trainees or practitioners. In fact, the short-term effects of personal therapy for the inexperienced resident may be negative; the trainee may become less spontaneous and more self-conscious in his or her work.

On the other hand, there are a few studies and many anecdotal reports that suggest personal psychotherapy may have a beneficial effect on both the resident and on his or her treatment of patients. Clinicians who have been in treatment may become more responsive to patients, more empathic, and more tolerant of difficult patients (Greenberg & Staller, 1981). Through experience as a patient in seeking and receiving help, the resident experiences first-hand that which he or she is attempting to learn. Such experience can be particularly helpful when the resident's own therapy lends familiarity with the kinds and intensities of emotion that his or her patients undergo in their therapy. Although such treatment can in this way be invaluable, the resident's own felt desire and motives for seeking personal therapy must remain its paramount indication. Thus, it can be a useful adjunct, but not the focus of residency training.

Elements of Core Curriculum

With the above considerations in mind, it is possible to outline the necessary elements of a core curriculum that would provide the minimal training in psychotherapy necessary for optimal function of psychiatrists, both those who plan to practice psychotherapy as a major theme of their careers and those whose professional lives will emphasize other aspects of psychiatry.

1. A thorough grounding in the basic science of psychodynamics is a cardinal requirement. Ideally, such education should begin in medical school, or even before, with courses and seminars on psychological development and functioning. However, since this kind of exposure to psychodynamic principles is by no means routine in medical schools, a residency curriculum must start from scratch. Clear-cut exposition couched in clinical terms and free from metapsychological cant is essential. In addition to an organized and systematic presentation of psychological development and functioning, an integrated exposition of psychodynamic psychopathology must be included. Coverage of descriptive phenomenology alone, as exemplified by DSM-III diagnostic categories, is insufficient to acquaint the resident with the psychodynamic features that characterize the various syndromes.

2. Didactic seminars should be accompanied by clinical examples, preferably illustrated by either live interviews or videotape recordings. These methods are pedagogically necessary to illuminate "normal" behavior (developmental stages, "healthy" defenses, etc.), as well as to show pathology.

3. Special attention should be paid to the application of psychodynamic theory, to the understanding of nondynamic modalities of psychiatric treatment, both biological and behavioral, as well as to group process and administration. It is equally important to explore nondynamic factors operating in dynamic treatment modalities (e.g., learning theory or sociologic paradigms).

4. In a core curriculum, experience and training in dynamically informed supportive psychotherapy and brief

symptom-relief-oriented psychotherapy are essential. Although therapeutic contact with chronic schizophrenics provides a "laboratory" for learning psychodynamics and teaches important patient management skills to the beginning resident, exposure to such patients will not provide the opportunities to develop these other psychotherapeutic skills that permeate so much of psychiatric practice. Training in more intense, long-term exploratory psychotherapy may be provided as an elective experience in later years of residency.

An illustration of this model is a program in which the residents spend four months during PGY-I on a psychiatry inpatient service. During PGY-II they are exposed for the first time in any systematic way to outpatients and to supervisors who are all psychodynamically trained and practicing with these skills. The residents spend halftime for the full PGY-II year in such a setting and become familiar with the psychodynamically oriented diagnostic process (in addition to the descriptive approach) and with once-a-week psychotherapy, using supportive and symptom-relief-oriented psychotherapy.

They may elect to spend 10 hours per week in the same clinic during the PGY-III year, doing supervised twice-a-week exploratory psychotherapy. They may continue such an elective experience in PGY-IV in the same clinic, when they are also expected to present case material in an advanced case seminar, which focuses on the therapeutic use of the therapist's evoked emotional responses.

5. There is an extensive literature on pedagogic strategies for psychotherapy training (see, for example, Balint, 1964; Colby, 1973; De Rosis, 1977; Eckstein & Wallerstein, 1972; Johnson, Snibbe, & Evans, 1975; Lewis, 1978; Thompson, 1979; and Zaro et al., 1977), and we do not plan to make specific suggestions in this area. However, we do believe that there are minimum essentials. Dynamic psychotherapy experiences should include patients of each gender with a range of ages, diagnostic categories, and socioeconomic back-

grounds. For example, in order to evaluate the suicidal risk, residents need to experience and learn the dynamic differences between the depressed obsessional character with suicidal rumination, the depressed hysterical personality disorder with threats of self-destructive behavior, and the depressed borderline patient with a pattern of impulsive self-mutilation. Supervision should be ongoing over a sufficient period to permit experiences of therapeutic movement in the various phases of the therapy.

6. Seminar instructors—and supervisors—should include experienced and psychodynamically oriented clinicians comfortable with various modalities of psychodynamic therapy, rather than narrowly based. In addition, practitioners of nondynamic modalities might participate in "interdisciplinary workshops," exploring cross-applications of principles.

As an example of fruitful collaboration, in one department with equally strong biologic and psychotherapeutic orientations, the director of psychopharmacology and his assisting staff are also each practicing psychotherapists. In weekly psychopharmacology seminars with residents, the history and dynamics of a case are first reviewed, prior to consideration of drug management. The appropriate psychotherapy supervisor is invited to attend the psychopharmacology seminar to provide clinical input and to participate in decisions about the use of psychoactive medication. This informal context for interaction provides an excellent model of the complementarity of psychotherapeutic and biological approaches to patient treatment and indicates to residents the relevance of psychotherapy to clinical practice, even from the biological perspective.

7. Planning meetings of participating faculty are extremely desirable, to enable integration of teaching and minimize unnecessary repetition or parochial focus. For instance, in one biologically oriented department with a strong clinical psychotherapeutic faculty, many of the full-time faculty may harbor an antipsychotherapeutic bias or

skepticism that gets transmitted to residents in didactic or research meetings. Regularly scheduled meetings of both full- and part-time teaching faculty (including the clinical psychotherapy supervisors) allow these biases to be discussed in face-to-face dialogue in the presence of the training director, with guidelines for psychotherapy teaching clearly spelled out. Such direct encounters may limit the deleterious effect of such biases and allow a more truly integrated teaching program.

The faculty must maintain a clear sense of the goals of such a core curriculum in order to prepare the resident to be a better *psychiatrist,* whatever his or her career direction might be, rather than to train him or her to be a skilled psychotherapist. Alternate career choices, e.g., psychopharmacology, research, or administration, must be fully respected and the program geared to enhancing these subspecialty skills through the content and attitudinal education discussed above, as well as through appropriate elective tracks. Only by respecting the complexity and pluralism of modern psychiatry and neither exalting nor depreciating psychodynamics and psychotherapy will the increasing polarization within our field be reversed and the values of psychodynamic sensitivity, as well as psychotherapy, enrich all of psychiatry.

REFERENCES

American Psychiatric Association Commission on Psychiatric Therapies, Chaired by T. Karasu. (1984). *The Psychiatric Therapies.* Washington, DC: American Psychiatric Association.

Arlow, J. (1963). The supervisory situation. *J. Am. Psychoanal. Assoc.,* XL, 576–594.

Balint, M. (1964). *The Doctor, the Patient, and the Illness.* New York: International Universities Press.

Blum, J. (1978). On changes in psychiatric diagnosis over time. *Am. Psychol.,* 33, 1017–1031.

Brown, P. (1985). *Transfer of Care.* Boston: Rutledge and Paul Kegan.

Caligor, L. (Ed.). (1984). *Clinical Perspectives on the Supervision of Psychoanalysis and Psychotherapy.* New York: Plenum.

Colby, K. (1973). *Computer Models of Thought and Language.* San Francisco: W. H. Freeman and Co.

De Rosis, H. (1977). *Working with Patients: Introductory Guidelines for Psychotherapists.* New York: Agathon Press.

Detre, T., & Weinberger, D. (May 23, 1985). The psychiatrist of the future will have to be a neurologist. Presented at the Annual Meeting of the American Psychiatric Association, Dallas, TX.

Doyle, B. (1978). Working assumptions: American psychiatry in 1990. *Report to the Graduate Medical Education National Advisory Council.* Rockville, MD: NIMH Psychiatry Education Branch.

Eaton, J. S., Jr., & Goldstein, L. S. (1977). Psychiatry in crisis. *Am. J. Psychiatry,* 134, 642–645.

Eckstein, R., & Wallerstein, R. (1972). *The Teaching and Learning of Psychotherapy.* New York: Basic Books.

Fleming, J., & Benedek, T. (1966). *Psychoanalytic Supervision.* New York: Grune & Stratton.

Foley, H., & Sharfstein, S. (1983). *Madness and Government.* Washington, DC: Psychiatric Press.

Frances, A., Clarkin, J., & Perry, S. (1984). *Differential Therapeutics in Psychiatry: The Art and Science of Treatment Selection.* New York: Brunner/Mazel.

Freedman, D., & Gordon, R. (1973). Psychiatry under siege: Attacks from without. *Psychiatric Annu.,* 3, 1–134.

Gediman, H., & Wolkenfeld, F. (1980). The parallelism phenomenon in psychoanalysis and supervision: Its reconsideration as a triadic system. *Psychoanal. Q.*, 49, 234–255.

Giovacchini, P. L. (1975). *Psychoanalysis of Character Disorders.* New York: Jason Aronson.

Goldberg, R., Haas, M., Eaton, J., et al. (1976). Psychiatry and the primary care physician. *JAMA*, 236, 944–945.

Greben, M. (1976). Supervision of psychotherapy with psychiatric residents. *J. Can. Psychiatr. Assoc.*, 21, 141–144.

Greenberg, R. P., & Staller, J. (1981). Personal therapy for therapists. *Am. J. Psychiatry*, 138(11), 1467–1471.

Grob, G. (1983). *Mental Illness and American Society.* Princeton, NJ: Princeton University Press.

Gurel, L. (1973). *A Survey of Academic Resources in Psychiatry Residency Training.* Washington, DC: American Psychiatric Association.

Gurel, L. (1976). APA resident census data. In *Proceedings of American Association of Directors of Psychiatry Residency Training.* Hartford, CT.

Haupt, J. L., Orleans, C. S., George, L. K., et al. (1979). *The Importance of Mental Health Services to General Health Care.* Cambridge, MA: Ballinger Publ.

Johnson, C., Snibbe, J., & Evans, L. (Eds.). (1975). *Basic Psychopathology, a Programmed Text.* New York: Spectrum Publications, Inc.

Karasu, T. B. (Ed.). (1984). *The Psychiatric Therapies.* The American Psychiatric Association Commission on Psychotherapies. Washington, DC: The Association.

Karasu, T. B., & Bellak, L. (1980). *Specialized Techniques in Individual Psychotherapy.* New York: Brunner/Mazel.

Karasu, T. B., & Hart, S. (1979). Ballad on the past and future of psychiatry. *World J. Psychosynthesis*, 1(2), 26–30.

Karasu, T. B., Rohrolich, J. B., & Stein, S. (1978). A model for individual supervision in a general hospital. *Compr. Psychiatry*, 19, 323–329.

Keniston, K. (1970). Postadolescence (youth) and historical change. In J. Zubin & A. F. Freedman (Eds.), *The Psychopathology of Adolescence.* New York: Grune & Stratton.

Klerman, G., Weissman, M., Rounsaville, B., & Chevron, E. (1984). *Interpersonal Psychotherapy of Depression.* New York: Basic Books.

Kohut, H. (1971). The analysis of the self: A systematic approach to the psychoanalytic treatment of narcissistic personality disorders. In *The Psychoanalytic Study of the Child.* New York: International Universities Press.

Kovel, J. (1976). *A Complete Guide to Therapy.* New York: Pantheon.

Kroll, J. (Feb. 13, 1986). The importance of psychodynamics in residency training: A debate. Presented at the Twenty-Third Anniversary Meeting of The American College of Psychiatrists, Marco Island, FL.

Lasch, C. (1979). *The Culture of Narcissism: American Life in an Age of Diminishing Expectations.* New York: W. W. Norton.

Lazar, N. (1973). Nature and significance of changes in patients in a psychoanalytic clinic. *Psychoanal. Q.*, 42, 579–600.

Levine, M. (1981). *History and Politics of Community Mental Health.* Monterey, CA: Brooks-Cole.

Lewin, B., & Ross, H. (1960). *Psychoanalytic Education in the U.S.* New York: W. W. Norton.

Lewis, J. (1978). *To Be a Therapist: The Teaching and Learning.* New York: Brunner/Mazel.

Lewis, J., & Usdin, G. (1982). *Treatment Planning in Psychiatry.* Washington, DC: American Psychiatric Association.

Loewald, H. (1971). The transference neurosis: Comments on the concept and the phenomenon. *J. Am. Psychoanal. Assoc.*, 19, 54–66.

Loomie, L. (1972). Candidate and clinic problems in the selection of control cases. Presented at the Workshop for Psychoanalytic Clinics, Committee on Institutes of the American Psychoanalytic Association.

Lowenfeld, H., & Lowenfeld, Y. (1970). Our permissive society and the superego: Some current thoughts about Freud's cultural concepts. *Psychoanal. J.*, 39, 590–608.

Luborsky, L. (1984). *Principles of Psychoanalytic Psychotherapy.* New York: Basic Books.

Michels, R. (1985). The evolution of psychodynamic psychotherapy. *The Institute of Pennsylvania Hospital Strecker Monograph Series,* 22.

Morrison, A. P., Shore, M. F., & Grohman, J. (1973). On the stresses of community psychiatry and helping residents to survive them. *Am. J. Psychiatry,* 130, 1237–1241.

National Institute of Mental Health. (1978). Data on training grants awarded. Rockville, MD: Division of Manpower and Training, National Institute of Mental Health.

Nemetz, P., & Weiner, H. (1965). Some factors in the choice of psychiatry as a career. *Arch. Gen. Psychiatry,* 13, 299–303.

Nielsen, A. C. (1979). The magnitude of declining career choice. *J. Med. Educ.*, 54, 632–637.

Nielsen, A. C. (1980). Choosing psychiatry: The importance of psychiatric education in medical school. *Am. J. Psychiatry,* 137, 428–431.

Nielsen, A. C., & Eaton, J. S., Jr. (1981). Medical students' attitudes about psychiatry. Implications for psychiatric recruitment. *Arch. Gen. Psychiatry,* 38(10), 1144–1154.

O'Brien, J. P. (1977). Increase in suicide attempts by drug ingestion. *Arch. Gen. Psychiatry,* 34, 1165–1169.

Osmond, H. (1973). Psychiatry under siege: The crisis within. *Psychiatr. Annu.*, 3, 59–81.

Pardes, H. (1979). Future needs for psychiatrists and other mental health personnel. *Arch. Gen. Psychiatry,* 36, 1401–1408.

Regier, D. A., Goldberg, R. D., & Taube, C. A. (1978). The de facto U.S. mental services system. *Arch. Gen. Psychiatry,* 35, 685–693.

Reinhold, R. (Sept. 2, 1980). Government takes steps to avert glut of doctors. *New York Times,* p. C1.

Rothman, D. (1979). *Conscience and Convenience.* Boston: Little, Brown.

Sachs, D., & Shapiro, S. (1976). On parallel processes in therapy and teaching. *Psychoanal. Q.*, XLV, 394–415.

Schuster, D., Sandt, J., & Thaler, O. (1972). *Clinical Supervision of the Psychiatric Resident.* New York: Brunner/Mazel.

Smith, M., Glass, G., & Miller, T. (1980). *The Benefits of Psychotherapy.* Baltimore and London: Johns Hopkins University Press.

Somers, A. R. (1977). Accountability, public policy, and psychiatry. *Am. J. Psychiatry,* 134, 959–965.

Strupp, H. H., & Binder, J. L. (1984). *Psychotherapy in a New Key: A Guide to Time-Limited Dynamic Psychotherapy.* New York: Basic Books.

Thompson, M. (1979). *A Resident's Guide to Psychiatric Education.* New York: Plenum.

Yager, J. (1974). A survival guide for psychiatric residents. *Arch. Gen. Psychiatry,* 30, 494–499.

Zaro, J., Barach, R., Nedelman, D. J., & Dreiblatt, I. (1977). *A Guide for Beginning Psychotherapists.* New York: Cambridge University Press.

GAP COMMITTEES AND MEMBERSHIP

COMMITTEE ON ADOLESCENCE
Silvio J. Onesti, Jr., Belmont, Mass.,
Chairperson
Ian A. Canino, New York, N.Y.
Warren J. Gadpaille, Denver, Colo.
Michael G. Kalogerakis, New York, N.Y.
Clarice J. Kestenbaum, New York, N.Y.

COMMITTEE ON AGING
Gene D. Cohen, Rockville, Md., Chairperson
Eric D. Caine, Rochester, N.Y.
Charles M. Gaitz, Houston, Tex.
Gabe J. Maletta, Minneapolis, Minn.
Robert J. Nathan, Philadelphia, Pa.
George H. Pollock, Chicago, Ill.
Kenneth M. Sakauye, Chicago, Ill.
Charles A. Shamoian, White Plains, N.Y.
F. Conyers Thompson, Jr., Atlanta, Ga.

COMMITTEE ON CHILD PSYCHIATRY
Theodore Shapiro, New York, N.Y.
Chairperson
Paul L. Adams, Galveston, Tex.
James M. Bell, Canaan, N.Y.
Harlow Donald Dunton, New York, N.Y.
Joseph Fischhoff, Detroit, Mich.
Joseph M. Green, Madison, Wis.
John F. McDermott, Jr., Honolulu, Hawaii
John Schowalter, New Haven, Conn.
Peter E. Tanguay, Los Angeles, Calif.
Lenore F.C. Terr, San Francisco, Calif.

COMMITTEE ON COLLEGE STUDENTS
Kent E. Robinson, Towson, Md., Chairperson
Robert L. Arnstein, Hamden, Conn.
Varda Backus, La Jolla, Calif.
Harrison P. Eddy, New York, N.Y.
Myron B. Liptzin, Chapel Hill, N.C.
Malkah Tolpin Notman, Brookline, Mass.
Gloria C. Onque, Pittsburgh, Pa.
Elizabeth Aub Reid, Cambridge, Mass.
Earle Silber, Chevy Chase, Md.
Tom G. Stauffer, White Plains, N.Y.

Harold I. Lief, Philadelphia, Pa.
Carol Nadelson, Boston, Mass.
Carolyn B. Robinowitz, Washington, D.C.
Stephen C. Scheiber, Evanston, Ill.
Sidney L. Werkman, Denver, Colo.
Veva H. Zimmerman, New York, N.Y.

COMMITTEE ON MENTAL HEALTH SERVICES

George F. Wilson, Somerville, N.J., Chairperson
Allan Beigel, Tucson, Ariz.
Merrill T. Eaton, Omaha, Nebr.
John M. Hamilton, Baltimore, Md.
W. Walter Menninger, Topeka, Kans.
Jose Maria Santiago, Tucson, Ariz.
Herzl R. Spiro, Milwaukee, Wis.
William L. Webb, Jr., Hartford, Conn.
Jack A. Wolford, Pittsburgh, Pa.

COMMITTEE ON PREVENTIVE PSYCHIATRY

Stephen Fleck, New Haven, Conn., Chairperson
Viola W. Bernard, New York, N.Y.
Stanley I. Greenspan, Rockville, Md.
William H. Hetznecker, Philadelphia, Pa.
Richard G. Morrill, Boston, Mass.
Harris B. Peck, New Rochelle, N.Y.
Naomi Rae-Grant, Hamilton, Ontario
Anne Marie Wolf-Schatz, Philadelphia, Pa.

COMMITTEE ON PSYCHIATRY AND THE COMMUNITY

Kenneth Minkoff, Woburn, Mass., Chairperson
C. Knight Aldrich, Charlottesville, Va.
H. Richard Lamb, Los Angeles, Calif.
John C. Nemiah, Hanover, N.H.
Rebecca L. Potter, Tucson, Ariz.
Alexander S. Rogawski, Los Angeles, Calif.
John J. Schwab, Louisville, Ky.
John A. Talbott, Baltimore, Md.
Charles B. Wilkinson, Kansas City, Mo.

COMMITTEE ON PSYCHIATRY AND LAW

Jonas R. Rappeport, Baltimore, Md., Chairperson
Park E. Dietz, Charlottesville, Va.
John Donnelly, Hartford, Conn.
Carl P. Malmquist, Minneapolis, Minn.
Herbert C. Modlin, Topeka, Kans.
Phillip J. Resnick, Cleveland, Ohio
Loren J. Roth, Pittsburgh, Pa.
Joseph Satten, San Francisco, Calif.
William D. Weitzel, Lexington, Ky.
Howard V. Zonana, New Haven, Conn.

Henry J. Gault, Highland Park, Ill.
Judith H. Gold, Halifax, Nova Scotia
Roderic Gorney, Los Angeles, Calif.
Martha J. Kirkpatrick, Los Angeles, Calif.
Perry Ottenberg, Philadelphia, Pa.
Kendon W. Smith, Piermont, N.Y.

COMMITTEE ON THERAPEUTIC CARE
Milton Kramer, Cincinnati, Ohio., Chairperson
Bernard Bandler, Cambridge, Mass.
Thomas E. Curtis, Chapel Hill, N.C.
Robert W. Gibson, Towson, Md.
Donald W. Hammersley, Washington, D.C.
William B. Hunter, III, Albuquerque, N.M.
Roberto L. Jimenez, San Antonio, Tex.
Melvin Sabshin, Washington, D.C.

CONTRIBUTING MEMBERS
John E. Adams, Gainesville, Fl.
Carlos C. Alden, Jr., Buffalo, N.Y.

Eric A. Baum, Akron, Ohio
Spencer Bayles, Houston, Tex.
C. Christian Beels, New York, N.Y.
Elissa P. Benedek, Ann Arbor, Mich.
Sidney Berman, Washington, D.C.
Wilfred Bloomberg, Cambridge, Mass.
H. Keith H. Brodie, Durham, N.C.
Charles M. Bryant, San Francisco, Calif.
Ewald W. Busse, Durham, N.C.
Robert N. Butler, New York, N.Y.

Eugene M. Caffey, Jr., Bowie, Md.
Paul Chodoff, Washington, D.C.
Ian L.W. Clancey, Ontario, Canada
Sanford I. Cohen, Boston, Mass.

James S. Eaton, Jr., Washington, D.C.
Lloyd C. Elam, Nashville, Tenn.
Stanley H. Eldred, Belmont, Mass.
Joseph T. English, New York, N.Y.
Louis C. English, Pomona, N.Y.

Sherman C. Feinstein, Highland Park, Ill.
Archie R. Foley, New York, N.Y.
Daniel X. Freedman, Chicago, Ill.

Alexander Gralnick, Port Chester, N.Y.
Milton Greenblatt, Sepulveda, Calif.
Lawrence F. Greenleigh, Los Angeles, Calif.
Jon E. Gudeman, Lexington, Mass.

Seymour L. Halleck, Chapel Hill, N.C.
Stanley Hammons, Lexington, Ky.
J. Cotter Hirschberg, Topeka, Kans.

Jay Katz, New Haven, Conn.
James A. Knight, New Orleans, La.
Othilda M. Krug, Cincinnati, Ohio

Alan I. Levenson, Tucson, Ariz.
Ruth W. Lidz, Woodbridge, Conn.
Orlando B. Lightfoot, Boston, Mass.
Reginald S. Lourie, Chevy Chase, Md.
Norman L. Loux, Sellersville, Pa.

John A. MacLeod, Cincinnati, Ohio
Leo Madow, Philadelphia, Pa.
Charles A. Malone, Cleveland, Ohio
Peter A. Martin, Lake Orion, Mich.
Ake Mattsson, Danderyd, Sweden
Alan A. McLean, Westport, Conn.
David Mendell, Houston, Tex.
Roy W. Menninger, Topeka, Kans.
Mary E. Mercer, Nyack, N.Y.
Derek Miller, Chicago, Ill.

Joseph D. Noshpitz, Washington, D.C.

Charles P. O'Brien, Philadelphia, Pa.

Bernard L. Pacella, New York, N.Y.
Herbert Pardes, New York, N.Y.
Norman L. Paul, Lexington, Mass.
Marvin E. Perkins, Salem, Va.
Betty J. Pfefferbaum, Houston, Tex.
Charles A. Pinderhughes, Bedford, Mass.

David N. Ratnavale, Bethesda, Md.
W. Donald Ross, Cincinnati, Ohio
Lester H. Rudy, Chicago, Ill.
George E. Ruff, Philadelphia, Pa.

David S. Sanders, Los Angeles, Calif.
Donald J. Scherl, Brooklyn, N.Y.
Kurt O. Schlesinger, San Francisco, Calif.
Charles Shagass, Philadelphia, Pa.
Miles F. Shore, Boston, Mass.
Albert J. Silverman, Ann Arbor, Mich.
Benson R. Snyder, Cambridge, Mass.
David A. Soskis, Bala Cynwyd, Pa.
Jeanne Spurlock, Washington, D.C.
Brandt F. Steele, Denver, Colo.
Alan A. Stone, Cambridge, Mass.
Robert E. Switzer, Dunn Loring, Va.

Perry C. Talkington, Dallas, Tex.
Bryce Templeton, Philadelphia, Pa.
Prescott W. Thompson, Beaverton, Oreg.
Joe P. Tupin, Sacramento, Calif.
John A. Turner, San Francisco, Calif.

Gene L. Usdin, New Orleans, La.

Warren T. Vaughan, Jr., Portola Valley, Calif.

Andrew S. Watson, Ann Arbor, Mich.
Bryant M. Wedge, Washington, D.C.

Joseph B. Wheelwright, Kentfield, Calif.
Robert L. Williams, Houston, Tex.
Paul Tyler Wilson, Bethesda, Md.
Sherwyn M. Woods, Los Angeles, Calif.

Kent A. Zimmerman, Berkeley, Calif.
Israel Zwerling, Philadelphia, Pa.

LIFE MEMBERS
C. Knight Aldrich, Charlottesville, Va.
Bernard Bandler, Cambridge, Mass.
Walter E. Barton, Hartland, Vt.
Viola W. Bernard, New York, N.Y.
Murray Bowen, Chevy Chase, Md.
Henry W. Brosin, Tucson, Ariz.
John Donnelly, Hartford, Conn.
O. Spurgeon English, Narberth, Pa.
Stephen Fleck, New Haven, Conn.
Jerome Frank, Baltimore, Md.
Robert S. Garber, Osprey, Fl.
Paul E. Huston, Iowa City, Iowa
Margaret M. Lawrence, Pomona, N.Y.
Harold I. Lief, Philadelphia, Pa.
Morris A. Lipton, Chapel Hill, N.C.
Judd Marmor, Los Angeles, Calif.
Karl A. Menninger, Topeka, Kans.
Herbert C. Modlin, Topeka, Kans.
John C. Nemiah, Hanover, N.H.
Mabel Ross, Sun City, Ariz.
Julius Schreiber, Washington, D.C.
George Tarjan, Los Angeles, Calif.
Jack A. Wolford, Pittsburgh, Pa.
Henry H. Work, Bethesda, Md.

BOARD OF DIRECTORS

OFFICERS

President
Michael R. Zales
Edgewood Drive
Greenwich, Conn. 06830

President-Elect
Jerry M. Lewis
Timberlawn Hospital
P.O. Box 270789
Dallas, Tex. 75227

Secretary
Allan Beigel
30 Camino Español
Tuscon, Ariz. 85716

Treasurer
Charles B. Wilkinson
600 E. 22nd Street
Kansas City, Mo. 64108

Board Members

Roger Peele
John J. Schwab
John A. Talbott
Lenore F.C. Terr

Past Presidents

*William C. Menninger	1946–51
Jack R. Ewalt	1951–53
Walter E. Barton	1953–55
*Sol W. Ginsburg	1955–57
*Dana L. Farnsworth	1957–59
*Marion E. Kenworthy	1959–61